small boat

Winner of the Iowa Poetry Prize

small boat

poems by LESLE LEWIS

UNIVERSITY OF IOWA PRESS Ψ *Iowa City*

University of Iowa Press, Iowa City 52242
Printed in the United States of America
Design by Richard Hendel
http://www.uiowa.edu/uiowapress

The publication of this book was generously supported
by the University of Iowa Foundation.

Printed on acid-free paper

Library of Congress Cataloging-in-Publication Data
Lewis, Lesle.
Small boat: poems / by Lesle Lewis.
    p.   cm.—(The Iowa poetry prize)
ISBN 0-87745-839-1 (paper)
I. Title. II. Series.
PS3612.E849 S63 2003
811'.54—dc21   2002035377

03 04 05 06 07 P 5 4 3 2 1

For Dan & Hannah

Contents

Acknowledgments

I am grateful to the editors of the following
magazines in whose pages some of these poems
first appeared: *American Letters and Commentary*,
Barrow Street, *Northern New England Review*, *Old Crow*,
Mudfish, *Shampoo*, *Slope*, *Untitled*, and *LIT*.

small boat

Site 29

I don't know if you're interested in turtles, but three painted turtles lie on a rock, no six with their reflections.

Now four, no eight.

Now five, no ten.

Now six, no twelve.

The rich must remember the poor and the poor remember the beautiful.

Behind the Curtain

She goes to Italy, to Teaneck, to Afghanistan, and Walpole and then her hands over her head and then she takes her feet off the ground. It is someone else's life she thinks.

She flies past John Blair's and hears such wailing noises she's afraid they are killing pigs today.

She thinks elsewhere.

Here's one degree of warmth.

Here a cat sleeps on a dog bed, a mistranslation.

Here is modern androgyny and emotional flatness clanging.

Is there anywhere around here to go? The question is like a snowball on top of the Buddha's head.

Here is a spring garden, all green and birdy with one hundred learned canary birds. A girl and her peacock travel through dangerous mountains. A young man greets a new life aboard the banana boat. A baby lives with a mouse family. We are all headless and cannot speak.

She cannot believe there isn't even one brave and necessary thing more, just a sledding night behind the curtain of a café.

Ode to Spring

I have so many things to think about; I haven't thought about you.

You've renovated the basement.

This is remarkable.

River broken bits of crust edge break and bubble down.

Everyone is rushing to look at the meat of your cough.

I will be yours to love in the dog sleep.

Ode to the Cough

Without all the froufrou and humbled by obstacles, let it be revealed to you how to love boring snow, two feet on top of two feet in the act of finding some eau de toilette.

"Ten times more happiness," says the gardener, "If you can't lift your feet, drag 'em."

You rearrange the furniture in your head, but first the rooms to make a cozy sick room: vaporizer, water, spit glass, clock, the bed opened up with sheets.

I believe in my version of transcendence.

I'm less sure of the other.

"You have two weeks to tell your story and I'll hear no complaints about the deadline," god says.

Light in the Field

Sun like gun cracks descends.

We attempt to mouth the various shades of asters, vetch, truck tracks, and overgrowth.

The effort runs itself to the ocean and foams and froths and caps itself in immensity and does not, no never, rests.

Hearkening to the call, we want to leave our lives and go on without them.

It's an illness and we're not to blame for these times.

The Doctor Throws Some Vehicle in the Humors and the Patient Is Animated

The world is round on a bowl, a one-two-three egg.

One spoon wants what another has to eat.

Wealthy artists of Annisquam spend too much time looking at their canvases.

My mood is rain.

The work to do there is the dark, the list grows with each bout.

Driving to the ocean with the time I'm growing into, watching lightning from the porch with Marie's dogs, I'm suddenly younger.

I'm roselike.

When your face laughs, my mortar turns to rubble growing flowering succulents.

As a woman cradles a bunny, the soil is temporarily one with the breath.

And then we can say, "What a fair country!"

Ten Trees

Get the drill. Check the battery. One hand gestures to the other.

It's a single act of attention to recognize a maple and drill the hole. You think in birds or like the insides of a wild horse.

You use substance tools, whatever, a transparent wash and matches. From young trees sap runs with gusto.

Wiser trees consider running. You'll have to check back tomorrow.

You cross-country to Lily Pond rushing back to check the sap flowers.

The sap ping pings in the buckets like it's tomorrow.

You sit under a bear-clawed tree imagining other choices.

You hyperfocus on each dribble of seeping and each sip is bleeding.

Tomorrow will become no longer vacant.

Overnight, the running will stop. Meanwhile, put a woman, a man, and a hat in the picture. Also some flowers and a mule.

When We Grow Up We Want to Be Dreamers

We started out in a city and drew the buildings squarelike.

We became oppressed by all the rectangles.

Next we know we're out of town.

Tonight's the blue moon simpering into its radical own face.

We are four humans in the woods watching a porcupine.

We live in a more fortunate day.

Between us and the laurel bush, a fire and lots of smoke and snow behind the bush.

We don't have to notice.

The ache pours out our backs.

It's syrup when it's half the sweetness of molasses, when it ribbons, when it aprons from the dipper.

With no calm base to leap from, we leap, leaving the biggest trees around the house, making the windowpanes be small, and giving up handsomely.

Our Campus

Some amphibians are new at being old.

The invention of zero follows the discovery of nothing.

The handsome rooster poisons our colons.

Pastel trees, a woman's sharp features, and her neckline slip.

Over a cell phone on the public green, I'm too shy to say the cheese grater is already dying.

A Baby Crying on the Train

Your mind knows a lot that it doesn't share with itself and the ignorant part wakes up and goes exploring drawn to the open for gold.

There was a she-dream about it, and she spoke irrepressibly, ambitions secret to be the most beautiful girl you know.

But you are sick of beginner's mind, the way of powerlines running by, the yes, the pretty river.

The air moves rawly believing that feeling the dark is this hard boulder dropped into an otherwise unbouldered woods.

So in the end, the end hangs.

This Is Steaming Cow Dung

My poet friends have a magician's club. They understand a little of their art and then not and then yes and then not and then yes and then ultimately not. But the birds are quite clear in what they are saying: "You live and then you remember living."

I really would like a self with a period after the s, a self with adjectives like necklaces named in art or love: art as the slight avoidance of suicide, the man-approval-woman-approval-mother-and-lover combo, like a night you get to sleep through, what you have to do like the drink you have to have, a this-is-how-you-do-it poem, and love as in I will touch you with affection while riding from Vermont to New York on the ferry and watch ducks in formation and not what it looks like watching ducks in formation. You will walk halfway into the water, then dive. Perfect circles will form like perfect therapists. I will blur my eyes into a painting with you swimming in the middle. You will recognize my sex. I will learn to make the laughing sound.

Defining and dissolving are two yankings and all smarts crack open like a nut in the midsummer sun and dissolve like mountains don't want names. No longer the dot in the dark inside myself I'd find after the bath on the floor in the pattern of tiles, it's now the sun shedding its clothes at me, everything at once. The sun violates me while the raindrops spit on me and flies dive-bomb my head. I have to ask, "What is this?"

In Cricket Season

Our bodies are flowers, our legs the double stems, our chests the petals, smoothed down and back like feathers, our heads the emerging seedcases, so smooth we can't get in or out. Nothing is graspable, nothing is perfect, nothing is ever finished for certain.

If we let go of our seeds, bronze, paper, fanned air, daughters, olives, knees, an ivy-framed window, reincarnation, spiders, male from female, an old man's young male nurse, we will be empty. If we have to, we'd like to at least give them up grandly, like two million happy people, like young salmon released, like the number of notes sung to one syllable, multiplied and multiplied, the melody most "spiritual."

We wobble forward on our stems, our leaves the hands to make stews, cheeses, our own arrangements, a campfire. The fire finally cracks our heads open and our seeds sprinkle around our feet. Surrender.

We breathe in the flames smoky and wild.

It's very gentle and quiet and our skulls are left wide and completely eased.

Our flower bodies take their thousand year naps.

There's heaven after heaven.

We have our own fields to moonbathe.

We love every star.

April House

April is a generous house, a high heaven inclination to be a body with a toothy smile riding no-handed the beast of a bicycle whose two wheels let the mourning get done before the loss and the windows shut.

Waltz of the Wood Thief

ONE

In search of counsel and kindness, our house crosses the bridge to the park, the dog's bark, the monument.

It is the first time our house is sad and most inarticulate about his trust in the hammer of his construction.

The house is rough to his own feel like late fall dusks fall, and even the first bugs and blossoms.

In trying to feed and be kind to himself, he realizes that he is not kind.

He becomes happier in the silence of the pines that house birds he has ventured into.

We let the house when it's quiet be quiet.

We open the refrigerators of our hearts and take out the bacon.

We sleep around if that's what it takes to be warm in the pits of our pajamas.

TWO

You live in a long house of rooms each with its own clarinet; that's how the memory tastes.

Like when the real ghosts of your parents came to visit, tonight you have some real anxiety.

A train whistle wishes you well well well but your mood is not improving.

The physical world needs to stand up and slap you!

Cardinals flit around your teacher's ears like more cardinals in the snow on the cliffs under the George Washington Bridge.

How your face would look without all the hair is a birch tree, and a man in a red jacket I can see through your branches is your rosy mouth.

Coffee does its curve-ball and clears your thoughts so they at least appear clear to the side that stands outside.

One clear thought is one person skiing in the woods who meets a wood thief.

For my traveling companion I take you a dog; we'll whittle away at the silence wood with a reassurance that rides a bicycle original untranslatable.

If you see a red cape on a woman out the window in the blizzard, she's me; I tell you I'm home.

Who does not want to be loved like the snow falls and embraces evenly the earth and every branch of every tree?

THREE

They say "the value of adversity."

Is it nothing but that bark in the dark, a problem, a pill on a pillow out to float?

Is it Uncle John's soul hitting the white walls in squares?

How it disappears off the high walls in a waltz!

In a dream of repose under drama clouds he meets the guilty and tells them they are not guilty of ambition or suicide or anything.

They can, he says, raise their own beings to higher levels so finally they become great enough to overflow their barriers.

In the wood ravines where it is complicated and snowing he comes upon a tepee.

(The outsider doesn't have a job and his days pass just fine.)

Faint birds sing a meditation into warmer soil pockets.

Is there a teacher for it, the flowers of it?

FOUR

The driveway is too long to shovel.

Unreal computer tables are also not your dream discussion of hypertext.

Everything is hard about the snowmobile paths.

Winged theory could ascend but it would be too cruel to leave the faults of living flat behind.

I once saw a photograph of the soul rising in an abandoned agricultural area.

FIVE

There once was rain on the canal.

This morning is up to five degrees.

I am whining like a dog to go out, desperation in the bladder and the bark.

Look then to beyond to rest.

Fletcher's high snowfields are far from anyone who could possibly need anything.

Only deer have come to browse, reading what there is, walking what there is.

SIX

Over the top exhausting like a diebenkorn sky comes down, let me not
get worse sicker, complicity and the crying sister.

I am a storm horizon flat in your face as a house.

When we were four, I remember you couldn't handle the truth of death,
the depth of snow minus the fluff factor.

Now I offer my labor across white acres and to the river.

A springish party sighs in unison in romanticism and laughs in the valley.

The mission of their word birds with jumping legs is one fluffy puffy jelly
filled for me!

The Better Person That My Dog Taught Me to Be

I.

If your body is your art, I'm sorry for you. If you study people's lips. If one fluttering leaf across the pond is female, quick we must decide how to treat her. Is she to carry the burden of the seasons or to be decked and carried herself?

I could swim. It could rain. I love my wife. I let the cats in at night. It's a fixed but elongated happy time, the hollow place meant to be hollow. Eyes close and hop.

You keep pets, and you don't make scenes in a world full of Bellini eyes and Bellini's Fortune, the woman with the globe and the babies in a boat, and lovers causing the almond to suddenly white blossom. To be more than willing to give up friends and occasional health, choose the quietest room. That blue is a slate plate, that green is coming, that breeze is a clean bed, and I say there's no joy.

You ask harder questions to make sure you don't know the answers. A critic rubs the feathers from his head and in the moment sees me where I am at home with paragraphs and spaces between them and the pauses are taken over a dying dog.

2.

Each rock in the river is a dog. Each morning is in fog. Each person is a god. God is another word for longing, my god, my longing.

Be kind to people, smile and help them in little ways. (Because of #1, the ways are little.) Don't shoo away insects who want to land on any part of your body.

3.

It's a pauper evening and there doesn't have to be life or even a universe, the baby goat cries and cries and cries.

The place we ask questions is a patch of grass and ten minutes in which the blank weight of self has a period of pinkness.

Like an infant looking out the window, nothing whatsoever being certain, the crow, the crickets, the cat, we are that chirp of the nuthatch. How grand to be everything! What a way to live!

You can always open your mind wider. If the leaves turn early red, it's a red dress or a red car you're buying.

A phone rings and the person answering it says, "This is His Greatness and Her Greatness," then hands the phone to you. You put down your bag of sanity.

Rain to listen to, I wish it were only that.

An Hour Back

When you find the plum trees fenced with posts waving music CDs, the youthful forest, and the cows, skirt them.

Time is a rabbit.

Lie down and release this odd urge and odd doing.

The thought is a suddenly discovered small whole number hiding between the five and the six.

Time is a big number.

It's not an adequate expression.

There's still the juniper, the grass, the pines.

Still the sky ceiling when you open your eyes in the ward.

Still wind blowing weeds, scattered plops.

Still you.

I am a complete head done with its turmoil and thinking.

The Menders and the Breakers

The rain does not cool and is a sticky one to the present and the place.

Is it a weakness, yours for narcotics?

The trees levitate and become mountains.

You stand in the water inside a melancholy boulder.

Now you're a flying sandwich.

Sunlight on Interior Barn Wall

The woman in the doorway panics (feels panic).

Her ice heart beats.

"It's whatever you want."

She carries a small dictionary.

A reticule is a small net bag.

She works with her god-given nose to make and keep what she will lack and need someday.

The work is called Sun on Barn Wall because it's raining like the world without her in it.

A pink crabapple blossom drops onto the back of my hand turning the page of *ARTnews*.

If she never lived, I would tell her life is like a canopy of flowers.

Love in the Palm House

Dear orange flower, even if my romantic attraction to you is only the "antidote for our existential loneliness" airing the Palm House with some truth, shedding out and rebeginning against hunger, and opulent as a Christmas pie cooling on the counter, the reality of your blossom is forced to open while I watch. In what state is your white stamen single cottage soul? In Massachusetts where the scale is tipped, enlarged, beyond what I once imagined, your orangeness spreads. Not that you would know me as a new puppy might come to look at me with doggy eyes. It makes sense to sit with you and chew espresso beans. Orange flower, teach me to draw heaven; "Heaven is exactly in the middle of the chest of the man who has faith" (Dali).

You've put up with flocks of mortals. You don't need any stroke of midnight hugging madness to comprehend light when it is not on you. Oh, you are intelligent!

My Say-So

The muse holds between his two index fingers, the project: to record a peony for a millisecond in hyperfocus, fields and fields of days and days and days of fields, pinkest lupine surrounded.

My feathers, fish, and wine, my corn and my egg hang upside down.

My house is made of stairs and a window.

The ranger is a white-bucket weeder too.

Does he love his work among the pale yellow irises?

Young Lily

She's a vertically inclined hip flower, go gone a bit windigo crazy, lobster boat Charlie red hopping hot. Man, watch her grow! Self-lit, self-steamed summer bud sizzling stinging smooth, she knows how to move. She wears cool flower clothes, black white taps tops. There's no stopping her. She's a flower on the run, free of the spiritual, a bit cynical, uncertain, perhaps practical, unsentimental, politically concerned and correct if not active, but not personally concerned, not generous, self-conscious, an experimenter in a chaotic world, free, anxious. Nine was the perfect age. She knew it even then.

Blue Comma

House rolls into car.

A friend is so depressed he has to leave his girlfriend.

I remind him not to forget his umbrella and by this time the house has been towed away.

Can I say how tired dead I am?

It's a busy mind these days and hardly a heart, a nighttime of chairs.

Night is a time we know of from daytime experience.

We'd like working together.

No, we wouldn't.

We Love This Place Gently

The prince made a worried babyface and zipped his sweatshirt right up to his chin. The sudden descension of the season and its mood stayed until our company left. The dog thought we were all love machines. Our visitors' energy was shared and in the throat. I was a fortunate, sharing with the brothers. I was not the center of anyone's suffering universe even if I felt their pain always in my liver. My secret longing was for baby animals and wonderful drugs, a head (oh, it's mine!) floating. My prince paddled to the island of a neighbor, smearest paint. She was noticed finally; her train ticket was also her bookmark and her hairdresser.

The Lonely Arts Bug

1. With the most recent weather on West Fourth Street, I am irritable. It's you that makes it rain.

2. Hunched over concentration on the music. Man with truck to remove trees. Not to remain fixed and not to neglect self-development.

3. Put your arms out. Trees crash down, give you a good headache. Then we napped in the sheep meadow like we were drugged to the depths where fountains spring from stones. You uttered a waterish noise, "Kayak adrift, multi-bird, duck, deer, heron." The underwater, that was uttered too, the fierce black core curled like a Jackson on the bed.

4. You lie heavy on the couch by the window, your friends with the large hearts and disturbing large breasts, your big man tears, the last night of the little family, and the birth of pity baby.

5. Vault. Perfect. Bug.

In the Grove of Hares

Why should one tree bud quicker than I can carry my body home?

Quick as one number subtracts itself?

Why does only the head need a pillow?

New Hampshire Spring

"The purpose is to determine if the recording of experience is too easy or too hard," he said. He said, "I'm here to be looked at and I'm looking at you." He said that walking was the last thing on his mind, even when he walked. He believed me. That's good enough for me. That's all over me. I feel today the tailwinds of that man.

Life is not boring, just on pause between exciting things I can't predict. "Be mindful," people are saying. Go to. The car is full of gas too. The fun I have with you, I have with no one else.

So if there's a little rain and it's early April and your window is open a little so you can hear it and it is the first night of peepers and you are a little worried that your marble bookends will give way during the night and wake you with a terrible crash, then you know the terrible anxiety that your pleasure will end, your life will end.

A pale yellow body turns away. You watch the body turn away.

Fleeing Woman Looks Ahead

Gas station roof, gas station doors, and tar road are caucasian as sky, an impossible voice rising suicidally close to the edge of a balcony on the wrong side of a railing. Not a cosmic floral tragedy; the earth stops her fall.

There are two ways around the recovery spiral: the light of her brain popping electric pills and downstream's the world where buffle-head ducks swim in the wetlands and those darn invisible birds keep getting happier.

Summer Solstice

The sun is stuck in my socks.

It may be rainy tomorrow as well, but anyway it's cloudcuckoo land and those who bathe in it be them then drowned in the lake breeding reluctance in others to ask what the future might be.

The crops are growing.

Someone has died and left his hat behind and who should find it and wear it will be loved by everyone and all over love will spring forth like more and more green shrubbery and ferns.

The day is perfect.

The teenagers are happy.

The shops in town have wonderful things.

Me and Little Mister

When me and Little Mister swam under the stars, the water and sky got switched.

In the morning, we took a trip to the steamy city. We sang all the way. How silly were the minds of our running mouths!

The city was flattened space. I inside myself stayed because it was a little scary. Where was the booming morning?

We lived with Mary Beth. We told her the dead rats story but she was not made frightened. She ate a peach. Her dog licked our spreadable, butterlike toes.

Evenings, I made pancakes from things I found on the streets.

Then one Sunday Little Mister left town.

He waved good-bye with both hands. The town collapsed.

I folded up and became an envelope with a flat heart inside that said, "Be mine until forever." The letter which is me had no address. No one will ever get it.

In the Mind of a Dragonfly

I am what goes on in the mind of a dragonfly, that small and urgent. I take my bike to the orchard hill. I go to sleep there. I wake up. I am the wind, that big and invisible. I roll over. I am too hot. I walk. I am a path in the woods. I walk downhill to a farm with a pond. I see no cows. I walk uphill to my jacket and helmet baking in the sun. I am my jacket and helmet baking in the sun. I eat my nectarine. I am where my nectarine comes from far away. I am all the things I take the time for and what I am is not that important to hold onto anymore. I take off my shirt. I am my body in the sun. I think about swimming. I am the thought of swimming.

Burdick's Picnic Table

How it feels to sit here with a gun to my head! Snapping turtle eggs are unwanted like your boyfriend becoming a monk but not bad things unto themselves. The shepherd, the herd, and the chapel, tomatoes piled neat to the windmill, those bodiless hands, your geometric head, your limbs through the window . . . well, outside's much calmer: roads and roads and tulips.

A Dream Goes Out

Turn to page one hundred and in the turning let your wrist slide downward and in falling hit a bottom floor welcoming you the way a tender mother greets a child, takes her hand and leads her to a napping room where the shades are drawn.

A dream goes out into the world, dressed comfortably, feigning confidence, stopping at the first café. On Primrose Hill, the sun he sees is a clothesless man, but because of the rum in his coffee, he can't be sure.

We're now half in the world, the temperature perfect like two eyes reflected in the mug and one frog in the water pot. The glass that is in the blue window of the white house on the coverlet is plenty, so there is on the cobble a honeybee on clover. We understand with distant minds and even that is only a cow and a cricket. There are children to consider. Will they swim? Will they have straight teeth? Sometimes the ideas themselves get tired and we have to put them to bed while they are crying because they don't recognize their misery as sleepiness.

Our hearts stay full. They are worlds of red darning needle flies. The fields are hearts of beef cows. In the stethoscopes we hear majesty. The grazing is on clouds. Love is of the inner organs. The grasses move aside for baby truths. The right track we are on is a promise and not a deed done, but why get the deed done? The day swallows us and spits us out into Tuesday. Our limits we can and do dare exaggerate.

I Am Riding a Horse

We reach the hilltop in two hours and from now on come the words that come after. The words are Flagstaff and sadness, sleepless on mescal, drinking water, the Monte Vista rooftop at night.

The words that come before are desert hike, no water lost hot, horse bones, dog with an eye hanging out early morning on the bench with the begging puppies, waterfalls and water running.

The Havasupai come out of their houses in the morning, prop open their windows, and sit in their doorways.

I am getting closer to it. I am on the day of it. I have on the right clothes for riding.

The guide's name is Tam. He lets the packhorses run loose on ahead.

I am very close to it now.

Another Havasu joins us, lets his pack run on ahead without him. They hang behind. They pass the pipe. They ask me do I want a hit.

And this is it now, what I wanted to say. I am riding a horse with two Havasu between red canyon walls and the sky between the walls is very blue.

Ashintully

We have coffee on the fourth doric column of the ruins in the rain after the mansion fire burned the pleasure of a study and a print and frame shop.

Fog moves over the hills that don't move.

"Bigger thinking," says an invisible sayer.

It is the horses in the trees.

It is the moon over the hat.

At Ball Mountain Dam

Future children know their minds earlier, thankful for, not thankful to, the spirit of exhuberance injected into hothouse weaklings.

They dunk all the way under like fuzzyheaded ducks.

They like it.

They seem to be happy like baby boxwoods.

The Kitchen Light

What with the door flung open, heaven and trees live together now in the thumb of clock.

We become abstract, falling into the bubble thought of a train driving to your typical coin in the sky, living on a whacked-out horizon line.

Do you think the screen door is ripped?

Is the linoleum peeling?

We wax ecstatic by the window light.

Our legs have urges to go at it fiercely.

Falling

At the quarry, a serious person never seriously considered jumping into the water from this height, but she worried about her dog falling in, and *then* she jumped.

Am I jumping now?

This feeling bad has a name. He's called Falling, many choices and one destination. He's an unnecessary person and hot burning at the tip of the inexpressible. He is the fall from summer like looking out through venetian blinds. He is a falling man.

I carry three books at a time. They all end with coffee in town, a change stuck in change, my pockets full of feathers, the effects of caffeine and nothing to do.

A foreshadowing of books leans, no ends to hold them upright, not where the sun hits on the bed but the spot of blue blanket lit and I am the person waiting for it.

The west tree is the chestnut walking stick, the pillars of my house, and the bowl is nuts on my table, how I feel and it changes.

I carried the great man's books for him down the stairs in a box to sell after the reading. It was fall then too. It was November. Now it's September, a solitude if from which I could recover, I would want to see people again.

Chimney is house, wicker screen is pretty, daughter's half-portrait like from heaven smiles down.

On Derry Hill the blue sky behind the clouds is forever as long as I live, but it is only blue in the sky, the direction south in Tibet smart birds fly.

Snow, Paper, Love

Molded snow shows the shape of the earth and how long her love lasts.

She won't let you go back to the pile of you's that wears mirrors in place of faces.

To lament a lament that there isn't time, to wring some paper juice, her life is not opposite to the one involving a woman chasing a man around the globe.

The page in the sun, that whiteness, the fine-tipped shadow, the snow in shade, that blueness, are the spirits over all breezes in her ear, no child murders, not her mother's sins, no depression.

Different paper, not so bright, and softer, to invite a tasty ink, unfolds itself over her parents' picture as if it comprehended the temporal condition of its crumpled bunchedness.

Pictures from the Linden Farms Institute

I.

Old married lunatics make love like moonlight shining through icicles, his ears the moon halves.

Then they watch TV with a remote and it's a cold nine degrees out.

She has an extra blanket on her side.

He's barechested.

She falls asleep first.

A little later he turns off the news.

There lies in sleeping an abstract weather pattern in the eaves of dawn which never lingers long in the daytime, a pink light on that blue white snow on the woodshed roof.

2.

I feel neither thoughtful this morning nor not thoughtful.

"Non-writers would not know exactly what, in a writer's life, [such] a crisis looks like."

The hallway chandelier light temporarily resolves the conflict.

I am auspiciously alone.

There's pasta in the refrigerator, dirty dishes in the sink, another gustatory medium.

Yes, one between long and lasting.

You tell me what chore needs to be done because it never has and I'll set myself on it to please you, so precious in your maternal love you'd kill someone rather than share this, two sips left of coffee and stains on the rim.

3.

Don't be shy when you have to use the bathroom.

It's no thievery to use the toilet, the tub, the sink, the towels.

Messages from above ground come to you, slide down through the plumbing pipes and you lay them down, cover each with its own little blankie and a kiss on its inky forehead.

So it's an interest that counts when the temperature rises to above freezing.

How much interest is there?

More than more than enough if you go through the files.

It's not a meaningless hum from somewhere.

Don't tell me you know because you don't recognize a portrait of an artist when he's young and doesn't even know himself what he does.

4.

The snow caves in on the lawn, a little dictionary thing then important now but it's not remembered.

The trees have grown, the squirrels wild.

I may be as dull as I am dull ready for my afternoon nap on the couch.

Tell me the name of this day.

Quietly I want it.

If my face should slip down to my chest even still lifes might be in this, "apples, a bottle, and a loaf," the experimental veined pale hand "hi," conversations among dream people who are kind to each other and why shouldn't they be?

Can I have a glass of water please?

5.

Drinking in the afternoon at the institute a glass vase sits on the table all afternoon and the sun sets through it rather slowly while we talk about declining and the conditions of souls, those airy feelings, the yellow palette.

6.

Everything is not something else.

All the cells of my body will not die at the same time.

My hair will continue to grow for several hours.

The cells of my skin and in my bones will live for several hours.

The smooth muscles in my intestines will contract twelve hours after my heart stops beating so slowly as I am leaving the big house through the big front doors not into a dark cold drizzle but into a floating situation induced by an intravenous shot of valium.

The Butterfly's Daughter

In the glass cupboard, a reflection of exact leaves in clouded background.

At the sculpture pond who sits on the deck like a party says "With cream" in German and we all hold our separate secrets.

The fly is a human in its shorter form on the book you are reading about summer life.

The stillness of a work that might say shimmer like water but cannot, the pond like the day is also pretty still, and the breeze relief written as my efforts to seduce you.

Push the button in the center of your palm.

Your strangeness will work for you.

"Choose me!" the butterfly's daughter hollers, "Choose me!"

Walking through It on My Broken Hoofs

I've been a jolly girl dog horse for thirty years. I've lived in this field for the last fifteen. My owner is putting me down soon to save me from another winter but her reductionist behavior belittles both of us. If she must, then window trim, door trim, pictures hung in her house. But rather as long as she can get along without, my end. If she takes me down near a hole and a backhoe pushes me in, where from this? Heigh-ho. Let it be *her*, not me, put down with an injection of chemical love and buried in the field. Or let us be put down bloodlessly together, our struggles like tomato plants to avoid the frost over and for all.

Little One

Little Carriage Horse always whines to come in and be warm when the brain is too tired to see. What you call a daydream, I call a scarf.

Your head is too big. Your back is see-through. How low the horizon line. Death rides a horse.

The beaver pond pathetically intentionally unfrozen tells me that I am a little fatiqued, I am a little human.

But yet I am also a little happy for tomorrow, for the countryside blonde, her teacher's embrace, and all the suggested panorama of passing days, the land of "poetry and love."

There's a Purring of a Lonely Poet Kitten in My Ear

No one liked you but your brother Vincent who was killed by a dog. A brother is like a second flower, what hovers over the shoulders of a Mallarmé.

You can't make us see what you see, the hot afternoon like carpet cleaner, the leg upon leg like just another egg. The simile is a dog that has lost its mind and not its life.

But you know the happiness of your body. You know if the color green were to have the podium, leaves would not fall.

Boy, you are not alone. There's a whole bowl of pears, a summer pond teeming, actual poets, and perhaps a brief exhilaration for you, you crazy boy, you bloomer, in their presence.

A Wild Place and a Town

Town, where people get gasoline and coffee and milk, mail their letters and get their hair cut, and not a wild place where people break down.

In a silence that sounds like my drink tastes, calm like a sheet descended, my brilliant baby and my red car in redness and brilliance, red-faced and rebellious, are crushed.

Was I six? Was I thirteen? Was I only two when the novel got itself lost?

A white rose that blooms late by ignoring sense emerges fuller.

To be quiet out walking with a dog at the bitter end of afternoon, October, Sunday; Jesus is immortal. The dog is white. You walk around the lake. Why do we say "heart" when we don't know what else to call it?

What is the large animal dentist from New York having for breakfast at Murray's? What farmer is having his cows' teeth worked on rather than putting them down when they can't eat? That herd of horned cows surrounds me and knowing I will be stampeded, there is nothing I can do.

Of course, there are some things to accept in every day. The bed is a boat. Sky and water are the most of it. We only have a little land to live on. Life gets better as you get older in a lot of ways.

So now it's time to throw that blue, that yellow, and call you into the world doorframed and windowed with brightness. The story is recognizable but I can't worry if it isn't. It's a table leg, a mug, a boot, a stove door, a jacket. It's a kitchen bowl dark and white with a fire glow. It is my love lying on the floor.

Bait in the Havahart

Homeless, sleepless, headless, the landscape's snowy nudity stumbles into you deeply when you ride the long train into north country.

The skin dries, dreams turn off, silent hums stop.

Not totally happy stories gather at your feet:

> A woman jerking off
> or on a rope
> dressed killingly,
> you blew her
> kisses.
> Yesterday, today
> into the cold view
> she faded
> clothes first.

You put on your glasses and take them off endlessly to see the center off-center, imperfect stuff that grows over the ghosts, the running of two walls, green pink and in.

Oh cry baby cry.

The nuns of neither sex chant now so like heaven is real.

You mix it all up in the pot of your mind: what's a roofline, bright light enough.

You might not notice the sun if it didn't hit your face during your English lessons.

You inspire me.

You said we'd conspire.

With nothing to do now but die, you learn to use e-mail so that your daughters will receive your messages from beyond if they weep and creep through the crawl space and put their ears to the furnace.

What Art Has Become in This Year

From over New York and Connecticut north to Canada west through the wilderness to Russia and hovering over China, I drop and return to what you call self. I'll buy her a coat for winter, my body turned into a coat on a ride into the far reaches of how someone yawns loudly for attention. This is not the yawn.

The morning of day 1,414, the year 1921, the character, not male or female, thinks only of love and farming.

Vladimir's chair falls over with his jacket on it which is another obstruction to contentment.

Center takes a backseat to my stomach, photographs of the dying, the just dead, and the long dead. I watch a student with the newspaper. I can't see his head from here and that's how it is.

The view from Burdick's of the unschool school of artists from which these men rise and pull with them from the great depths of chair something intelligent is like the energy of gut it takes to have each day like flowers.

The White Triangle

All night I waited for you to saw off my head.

"Do you know how to do this?"

I'm still thinking.

By dawn, stuff the breeze blows off the trees touches down easily on the water.

A fish jumps.

We have a white triangle in our yard.

No one would tell us otherwise; we are gorgeous.

If the flowers are in our hair, they must be in our hair.

She Studies Algebra

If x to the third is a cube, x to the fourth is something else like you might say to someone "You're something else." There's no three-dimensional picture of it, the individual house of the soul. It's not epically large, only a few rooms; not reassuringly strong, the roof and siding and foundation all need repair; not consistently comfortable, it's cold in the winter.

Getting There

So much snow payment is our road's muddy mess and a bluebonnet breakfast with trains rushing along the walls.

If the world is our model, what's all that thumping in the carpool lane?

The bodies in contact with the depths of souls play piano with the truth which will not set us free on the broken shell of a beach of a building.

Ron's place is the one masculine ending for the day.

He makes for us little beers with cream.

A girl falls to sleep thinking, "forever, forever, forever."

Outside Philadelphia, a portion of pink of storm gathers like a body human can, strange happiness.

Three hundred and ninety miles south red buds on trees, the rain in Maryland.

Once we were depressed and this trip would have been scary.

68 degrees—the first dream is dead.

From Tom's tin shop through red dirt Southern Pines orange dirt golf country horse country Jesus country one dead dog and then another, Cheraw Society Hill trees have a living in composition, baby leaves in a light rain.

Georgia washes away the old voices, "destroying the spiritual growth of others to defend the integrity of our own sick selves."

Where is the line on the weather map that says there will be no rain?

Trucks mate like dragonflies.

Our northern selves unself themselves like Florida palms undress themselves like private dancers at the truckstops.

To Cock-a-Hoop

Through light, in light, Western light, through the light of the mind, the way a fish hangs in the shallows, just me and my dog looking around.

"Hey you. I want to talk to you."

Where my garden peaks it is the summer's and my chemistry, my close-up look, and I try not to squeeze it, to be a water-eater.

When it rains, the woods drink and drink and drive home drunk.

What do I want?

A pill or a reason, new insects found whether I kill them or not.

When someone calls you, love is in the hospital.

It's a good thing for him, and it's his drug, the emptiness where white fungus grows.

The opposite of all this is none of this.

I want a young man to call a young woman, an elegy for a June bug crushed at intermission on a leaf on a brick in the sun.

Did you know that I was waiting for you?

"How the bees love these hollyhocks!"

"Yes Grandfather."

In Love Fields

The awful season ends.

The thumper is blind.

Drop off the hardship crying; how it hurts the body!

Hear the geese.

We step long like a subtle flower, the head of thinking, the kind of thinking on a thing that we do on a thawing body of water or flesh, the pieces of the face fading, driving in a music car in a poppy field.

The Easter train derailment is cleaned up.

The tulip shop tries to find her way with us in the love world that has no one way.

Sugaring

February 20

Move the wagon, the rocking horse, the high chair, get to the buckets. Drag them by sled to the front porch. Go get some white donut buckets from the garage. Wash them out with bleach. Andy's made cement in them. Start looking at the trees. It will be hard this year in deeper snow. Go get the mail. The snowmobile won't start, so walk. Nothing worth walking for.

February 24

Go to Dunkin' Donuts. Get more buckets cheap one dollar each and while there get a bag of donut holes for Dan's office.

March 3

Call Joe. No drill until tomorrow. Peel the snowflakes off the windows. Burn them in the fire. Put the horses out into the deep snow field. Drill two holes with the hand drill. Slow. The holes damp but no sap running. Tomorrow, the rest of the holes, running or not.

March 4

The sun hazed over. Go to town with Hannah. Drive to Joe's. Pick up drill. Don't listen to music. Don't look for anyone in town. Go out and tap the trees. Work hard and have patience. Call it bravery and feel a little better. In the cold wind bringing in a storm fifteen more taps. Fran says it hurts the trees, like bleeding them. Clean out the barn. Bring in the wood.

GATHERING

March 7

The sap drips a little, have faith, faith, faith in where the mind almost disappears where the wind hits nothing fiercely. If life were always sweet and god statues living, if all barns were heated in the winter, then half the bed, the map of new worlds, half human, half ink would be a sweet lover in dreams like buckets running over. What might come with the boiling, not large beasts but brain matter evaporated being tired with uselessness and there might finally come repose.

March 10

Apples to the horses, clean out the barn. Shakespeare calls to talk about Shakespeare. Out again. All but the first two taps running. Walk with KC to Midge's to water her pretty lady violets. Home. Gathering. Here's the ping ping in the buckets. Crying for this oh miracle oh black fairy insect oh birdsong ain't so golden. Inside the bucket it's louder. Needing this like a transfusion, like losing ten pints was all the sugar. Pour and the holes cry for their buckets. Switch the logs from the cart to the house to have the cart to cart the sap and the logs to boil. Front porch sitting hallelujahs. Light incense in celebration. Let the ashes fall on the train schedules. Tonight, start boiling on the stove.

March 19

Drink taste what's done. Meanwhile clear the buckets out of the mudroom. Spread sawdust. Pick ice chunks out of the horses' feet. Get in wood. Bring in new flowerpots. Snowshoe around. Come home. Crawl into a nap. Wake up and collect frozen sap. Watch one drop fall for as long as it takes, the long labor hard birth from which the better child comes, meltingness to crawl miles and days for, a life for, repose for, wait for.

March 24

Deep snow on deep but warm enough the taps can't help themselves and run. Snowshoeing is the only way to get to the trees. It's been a hard winter on the fox and squirrels. Feel sorry for them, feel sorry for Dan, do not feel sorry for yourself that winter wood and watering are so long, people visit for too long, talk too long, the driveway is too long, the walk down light, up heavy with buckets. Rest. Look up. What blue is this?

BOILING

March 11

A modern library extraction. Sugar from its cell and you from yours. In reconsideration of fate and turtles, the shuffle of cards. So the pen drops eyes drop. The time is late exactly.

March 16

Love for lots of things, one feather, one clay bird, one fortune's wheel turned up for so short a time. Ah, but what was—it's syrup by now. Space runs out in the heavens, meager minds, whatever it is we are given with our birth certificates, whose beds we lie in, even our own, even the woods deep in snow, the buckets drowned in. Boiled too far. Gone beyond the goodness madness to the useless unbearable solid, oh sadness.

March 25

Sled in wood and sap and pans. Shovel snow out from the fire spot. Dig a place for a chair. Get a good hot fire going. Jamaican sleep, air, imagining ocean. Watch tiny black bugs eating the snow. Read a little Boethius, firework, order in the universe. Smell the smoke, hear a crow, look at the sky again. Watch the fire and forget you are in charge of it.

Pretend it is in charge of you. Sun melt fire boil make the hot syrup. Make it make it make it for blue heaven, make it for gods and bugs, make it for good New Hampshire people, make it with gratitude. Come to something so poor and sweet, your skin all tight around you, you can't live with it.

March 31

Already the sap bubbles by the fire listening to Bachelard. Drink water today. The dog rises from her busy night to visit to curl up in the snow with a vast amount of leisure. A bird is singing for you, who else? You dreamed a major event but you didn't know what it was or if it had already happened or was about to so try to spend the day slowly. Imagine the immensities we are lost in, what refuge from detail and the roar of days and weeks long spent. Find a dry rock to sit on down at the pond. Listen to the water coming in. Try to like people today in case you see any but try not to. Hike around the pond, hike back up. The snow's deep. Check the fire, split kindling, bring wood in, clean out the barn, wet heavy manure, check the fire, check the fire, check the fire, drink water. Several barnloads to the garden. The cart half in the sun, red plastic gas cans shine in the sun. Warm hot now take off hat. On hands and knees scoop sawdust off the icehouse floor to spread in the barn. You're half evaporated now so you don't mind. Take off gloves. Check fire. Add sap. Tend the fire. Tend it. Tend it. Love it, keep it living. Someday get barn boots. Gently pull winter hair off the horse. Stop. Just sit or the boiling will get nowhere. Don't move! Maybe you are a fountain, maybe you are syrup, maybe you are what is evaporating away, maybe you are a wife and mother. How would I know? Close eyes, listen to fire and crow, smell smoke. Go inside the body. She's different than you expected in there. She's taller. She lets her mind wander more. I don't know where she goes. She almost forgets to wake up and feed the fire. Take her inside. Take off her clothes. Take her to bed. Love her. Put dry red socks on her feet. Make her coffee. Send her packing, evaporated. Stop. Drink her coffee. Go back out and tend the fire. Be more quiet here alone, much less busy. Drink a shotglass of syrup. Tomorrow it is supposed to snow and I am the April-born fool thinking I am done now and can rest. Go get Hannah. Go to the bank.

Small Boat

We cannot escape winter without a moral, more powerful wings lifting us beyond the reflections of ourselves in our own propellers.

Brushing my hair and having a nightcap I can tell you.

No one chooses us for his or her team; see how they drink in the open bars.

When the soul also dies, turning back is a valid direction.

We frequent the marshy places and one day a small boat appears.

Planting

Weed. Take out rocks. Dig holes. Put in compost. Plant baby bird bones. Plant a lock of hair. Plant doll clothes and buttons. Plant all the gifts and things you keep around your house just to look at, but never look at, wooden alligators, silver pineapples. Plant the photographs of dogs you were planning to send to your friend suffering chronic fatigue. Plant your lists of books to read and letters to write and evening projects. Plant yourself a nightcap and plant your family too. And put in bulbs. Pray, wait, bear with composure, and possess your soul in patience. Attend, heed, hearken to, sit up for, hatch, spawn, and beget. Anticipate, foresee, premeditate, and plan for the skinny-legged winged child, the jump-up-and-kiss-me flower. Water if it doesn't rain.

Mowing

Mowing is work that keeps you from the fall into contentment which otherwise you might feel especially on hot sunny mornings at the pond. Mow a path to the garden. Mow in close to the beds. Trim by hand what you miss. It's hot, hard work, this, the framing, the voice that says, "I give my life to you with infinite trust." The plants say this and the baby squirrels say this. You say this aloud until you are washed away into a wide field, so wide either side cannot be seen from the other. Jump up and kick your feet out behind you. Move your body through the grass like a swimming snake. Keep your head low and watch out for the mowers.

Offering

With this jam cover your bread and take pleasure like you could trade this life in for another anytime. Eat bread, lie down at night, and work in the day. Repeat yourself your seasons. Enjoy a few visions of red leaves in the sun, a few skies to yourself. Have a child's day of swimming with certainty. Take the adult years with the hills half in cloud shadows across the lake. Then take age with its wide mowed expanse of lawns. Look around. You've worked well and you're tired. You don't have to leave your body because your body will leave you.

Ode to Boiling Sap Slowly

Who treats your illness Madam?

I like your stinking eyes and the smell slowly going sweet.

I love March sun almost best.

I love visiting birds.

I love how long it takes a strong body.

I like the circle of a warm world I make myself putting flowers in snow's hair as if she had a head of hair, a head at all.

I like tending fire with the stick figures and insects in relief following violence.

I like that snowshoe paths are three feet above me.

I love the shotglass of syrup at the end.

I love how I make it go even slower.

The Inclination to Be Gone

I'm leaving all of you like you were a train station in western April.

I'm looking for a place to settle, as in a giant house of butterblue, tired and willing as the living room floor, stretched out on my gray down side.

I'm stupid as a door.

I'm half open.

I roll myself.

There.

And now I can lie here and listen and try to sleep and almost sleep.

A dreamy pas de deux strolls down a flower garden path and leaves me alone, pinking flesh in dim easy light.

Simple question.

Is heaven temporary?

From the smell of pine and ripple of water to a body that can transcend its pain, happifying, this is a good enough place though I miss there being animals, sexy as a skunk's stripe, or even some lonely scholar in the throes of detecting quiddity.

Here is where something might happen, religious or physical or even mentally a snap.

Also present tense.

Conditionals and that's the season.

A relaxed solitary hum humming over the times turning the color
within a year closer to light green, removing the stone of folly from
my forehead, and quick curing my stupidity that has bothered me like a
tulip drooping into a comma shape not striving with supreme powers or
elsewhere in the wide world explains at least or demonstrates how love
is like orange seeds spit into the stream and washing down.

The inclination to be gone is done.

I'm tired of it.

It's not real.

Don't ask it of me.

It can't be time yet.

It's not that late.

East Acworth Composition

Train master, blur master, hand curves like a swan master, her head moves around like a moon.

He took her around the park. It was madness, aha!

The crack of light between buildings, a hair of doubt, joie de vivre for a second.

She laughed with her heart case and guitar.

I said, "Boy, it's nice out!"

And so, I'm missing a button.

THE IOWA POETRY PRIZE &
EDWIN FORD PIPER POETRY AWARD WINNERS

1987
  Elton Glaser, *Tropical Depressions*
  Michael Pettit, *Cardinal Points*
1988
  Bill Knott, *Outremer*
  Mary Ruefle, *The Adamant*
1989
  Conrad Hilberry, *Sorting the Smoke*
  Terese Svoboda, *Laughing Africa*
1990
  Philip Dacey, *Night Shift at the Crucifix Factory*
  Lynda Hull, *Star Ledger*
1991
  Greg Pape, *Sunflower Facing the Sun*
  Walter Pavlich, *Running near the End of the World*
1992
  Lola Haskins, *Hunger*
  Katherine Soniat, *A Shared Life*
1993
  Tom Andrews, *The Hemophiliac's Motorcycle*
  Michael Heffernan, *Love's Answer*
  John Wood, *In Primary Light*
1994
  James McKean, *Tree of Heaven*
  Bin Ramke, *Massacre of the Innocents*
  Ed Roberson, *Voices Cast Out to Talk Us In*
1995
  Ralph Burns, *Swamp Candles*
  Maureen Seaton, *Furious Cooking*

1996

Pamela Alexander, *Inland*

Gary Gildner, *The Bunker in the Parsley Fields*

John Wood, *The Gates of the Elect Kingdom*

1997

Brendan Galvin, *Hotel Malabar*

Leslie Ullman, *Slow Work through Sand*

1998

Kathleen Peirce, *The Oval Hour*

Bin Ramke, *Wake*

Cole Swensen, *Try*

1999

Larissa Szporluk, *Isolato*

Liz Waldner, *A Point Is That Which Has No Part*

2000

Mary Leader, *The Penultimate Suitor*

2001

Joanna Goodman, *Trace of One*

Karen Volkman, *Spar*

2002

Lesle Lewis, *Small Boat*

Peter Jay Shippy, *Thieves' Latin*